Far From Healing

Butter Flies

Made with ❤ on the BookLeaf Publishing Platform
www.bookleafpub.in
www.bookleafpub.com

Dedication

My *Sweet Little Devil*
Mumma, *This Is For You*

Preface

Hi, you can call me butter flies. I chose this name because this is my first step towards not succumbing to my fears.

Butter Flies isn't just a name—it's a declaration of owning my fears instead of letting them control me. It's a reminder that no matter how much my fears try to hold me down, I'll still find a way to fly.

This collection of poems is a reflection of my journey transitioning from a teen into an adult—one marked by fear, growth, and the loss of my dear mom that has shaped me. For much of my life, I've let my fears dictate my actions, holding me back from becoming the person I who could be. Within this collection lies the loud melancholic soul experiencing those fears, the decision to face them head-on and embrace their power rather than be consumed by it.

Each poem represents a step along this path—some steps tentative, others bold, but all deeply personal. They are fragments of the chaos and clarity that fill the spaces between the moments when the heart speaks louder than reason, and the whispers of hope in the face of uncertainty.

I've always believed that poetry has a way of drawing us closer to what is most difficult to express. It is a language that speaks directly to the soul, crossing the walls we build around our emotions. These poems are my attempt to release the things I've kept hidden, to shed light on parts of myself I once feared. They are my way of reclaiming my voice and inviting others to do the same.

In these pages, you will find fragments of vulnerability and strength, love and loss, the push and pull of becoming. They are mine, but I hope they resonate with you, the reader, in ways that feel both familiar and freeing. It is through sharing these words that I hope to inspire others to never shy away from the power of their own feelings.

Trigger Warnings : Please note that this collection contains graphic imagery, explores themes of loss, grief and emotional pain. Readers discretion is advised

Acknowledgements

I would like to thank my mom for being my source of love. Everything I write comes from love. I miss you, and I love you so much more than I can express in my poems. Thank you for being there for as long as you could, for always listening to my work, supporting my voice, and believing in me.

I thank my friends for understanding me and being there when times got rough.

I thank my younger self for keeping on, even when it felt impossible.

I thank my late grandpa and my late mom for knowing everything I was and believing in the goodness within me—even when I couldn't see it myself.

I am deeply grateful for all the love I've been given by my friends and family, who stood by me with unwavering hearts. To Felicity, Adeline, Shyraa, Gahyun and Sonali—thank you for being my constants through this journey and becoming my new family.

And lastly, I love you, Grandma. Without you, I would have never met Mumma. You are the best, and I carry your love with me always.

to the ocean behind me, I give a great hug.

Sweet Poison

Sweet ivy how poisonous pursuing you,
Haven't I let you slip through the crevices of my
fingerprints?
Yet I seem to call out to you in this rogue wilderness
Time isn't your well-played game

Can you quench my thirst of wandering into the
waters?
Dive into the walls they've forced around my heart
Your touch transcends all my woes,
a moment for I wait to be blinded to you

Nevertheless, goodbye
~ Love

Insomnia Confessions

The echoes i hoped to sound like love,
ricochet violently the blood in my veins

I stay awake welcoming the moon,
Hit me with the darkness of my heart

Smear her blood on my face,
Run me through water so holy

Cleanse the corners of her despair,
Listen to her tears drop into the silence of my screams

Stop her from running into my arms,
I'll think about this fate another day at my funeral

~ 19 of some year

I confess the crime has been committed;
The voices have grown louder.

Her.

How do I even describe her?
She's an angel from heaven who walks on earth.
She's got wings but she loves to swim.
Her eyes—within her eyes I see the whole universe.
She's so beautiful,
I'd stand between the heaven and earth for her.
So pure, is her soul—
If there is anything purer than the heavens, it's her heart
and soul.
I love her, I cherish her love.
She's more than, than what meets the eye.
She's a story—a love story, a true story, an unfolding
story, a story of mystery, with a hint of horror—
But the kind that would touch you in ways you never
knew you could be revealed.
She's blood red, she's sage green,
She's the shades of colors you can see but never name.
She heals your soul, your skin, your heart.
*She'll love you in ways that you'd forget
you ever hated yourself or anyone else on this planet.*

She is me,
she is *you*.

Dear Time,

You sing a song I no longer recognize,
Every moment passing like wind through my hair,
I can't seem to hold it within my palms.
I trace the moment with the actions from a memory,
chasing the ghost of actions never taken.
Future calls to me, I wait at the station for the bullet
train to take me to the past to that 1 moment of tranquil.

You blindsided me, you sent *present* to the doorstep
I shut it close, for a stranger is out waiting to take me
away,
But my mom always said, "don't open the door for
strangers"
I hold onto a plate of *yesterday's* sorrows—oozing with
forgetfulness.

Too busy to go for a *tomorrow*
Yet, now the past haunts me from taking a step towards
the cold chai waiting for me
As I finally made my way to it, my lips touch the brim—

the chai touches me frozen,
I sit mourning the morning, my tears welcome you as
you are now
While I remain elsewhere in *another time.*

you still exist here

I have buried you too deep inside my heart, and I cannot dig you out now.

I do not wish to.

I do not wish to.

Not today, not tomorrow, not forever in the future.

I buried you deep inside my heart.

I may forget you within the fog in my brain,

And the deeper you seep inside,

But I will always refuse to dig you out.

Because if I dig you out, all those walls around you will break.

Everything I entrapped you within, will pierce into my skin as it shatters,

And I will have to let you go.

Once I dig you out from the deepest core of my heart,

All it will do is hurt me.

The pain would consume my body,

And the thought of being alive would not make sense.

Not today, not tomorrow, nor forever in the future.

I will crawl into the waters,

And the water will sting the wounds.
My cries and screeches—it will muffle, but only my heart
will hear.
And you will be living, with a smile and a joke,
For you have already forgotten me in the midst of my
liberation.
So, I shall not dig you out.
Not today, not tomorrow, nor forever in the future.
Yet, once in a while, I shall dive into this core,
Swim all the way through, defying the pressure that
inevitably compresses me.
I will dive deep into that depth,
To touch you, to feel your presence,
To live those moments with you once again,
Like you're still mine, and time is flowing only for those
moments.
But soon, I will have to swim back out.
Because if I stay there and time starts flowing again,
I will forever be stuck in the core of my heart.
Nothing would bring me back—
Back to life.
My body would turn to flames and become ashes,
And so would this flesh of mine.
But I would remain in this core, near your memories—
In this beating heart of mine.
Today, tomorrow, and forever in the future.

Just a story?

She sits on stars, watching the moon.
They talk for hours as she jumps from one meteor to
another.
But his eyes are always stuck on her.

From every angle the sun shines on her glistening skin,
the moon wraps himself in the warmth of her beauty—
with pride that she is his and with love in his eyes,
holding onto her presence from every reflecting ray.
He knows that she will never tire of jumping on meteors
just to talk to him about every little detail of her life and
the dreams she has to fulfill.

Yet the pain of never having touched her, the sorrow of
never having her land on him still lingers as he
remembers her while you look at him remembering your
lover.
But soon, she needs to leave, for she has dreams—for the
same reason the sun must set.

Even when she needs to travel a little far, he draws close
to her, fighting the gravity—giving us light in the night,
reminding you that the pain, the wait, and the want are
worth it... or is it?

Her tears fall like glitter on his face as she runs away
from one star to another, for something dire waits for
her on the other side.
He'd run crashing every planet after her if only his fate
wasn't to give us light during the darkest nights.
He radiates forevermore, waiting for her return.

And if this is all but a story, then so shall it be.

7. To the love who hasn't met me yet

Dear,

Are you miles away, across the seas, finding a beautiful
life for me?
Building a home that will cherish and hold our love,
for our families to explore?
Selecting the frames for our monthly family pictures,
the ones that will hang on the wall of "Best Picture of the
Year"?
Painting the walls of the room red,
a space that will store beautiful memories?
Are you light-years away? Or just miles?
Because it feels like forever...
They say I'll always love you from the bottom of my
heart,
but I fear that I'll push you off the cliff—because that's
what I do.
Will you let go of my hand?
I've been waiting for you,
cleaning and decorating my heart,

creating a home in it that runs in blood,
to quench your thirst.
Will you live in me, or tear me apart?
~ With love, from the *edge*.

Master, Are you sorry?

My heart isn't a stone,
I can feel the beat,
I can feel the blood rush to its commander,
Oh Master, My Master this heart beats for you.

A stone doesn't mold like clay,
I can feel this compression,
I can feel this agony,
Oh Master, My Master this heart bleeds for you.

Your sword has pierced through me,
I can feel,
I can feel what thou eyes don't see,
Oh Master, My Master this heart waters your life.

Oh Master, My Master my heart isn't a stone.

pearl

She'd wipe the tears off my eyes,
She'd drop them into the ocean,
Guide them to the oysters,
She made them Pearls!

She wore them on her neck, on her sleeves,
Hid the painful and precious ones in her heart,
She told her they're jewels of my suffering
She respected my heart for all it felt.

Yet she left again and again and again,
harvesting pearls, trying her best to show me what i can
be,
but i rubbed sand over my eyes, cried every time she had
to leave, covered my wounds with salt
With time as i grew weary, i stopped waiting.

Then came the day where she waited and waited for me
to come to her,
I ran away with the waves in my entangled hair,

I held her one last time as she breathed in my arms, as
my heart swelled I let her go,
OH How I wish I had held her longer—For a Lifetime.

This is what her heart read, *"I make them into pearls my
darling, to show you that every drop of water in your
body is worth it,
of your love and the sadness too, but never worth for it
to endure the torture that you endure, and the ones you
intentionally put yourself through, my darling I hope
one day you'll come through"*

Dear mom,

I wish you died back when you had your last best day
I wish you didn't have to get married to become the prey
I wish you saw the heaven earlier
I wish even before I was born you were in Paradise
Because every time I see those eyes I feel the fire that
burned you
I feel the pain you felt
I see the screams that shunned you
Because every time I look at my face
I see the other person in me who isn't you
The one who caused you the pain
The one who made you want to die every single day
I wish we had met in heaven not as mother and daughter
but just as a lady and child
Because we'd still learn to love each other
We'd still become mom and daughter
But this time I would only see love in your eyes
This time I would only see your parents
Because this time you won't have met the monster
And I wouldn't have known him either.

Dented

she said, "this can't go on forever"
she wasn't giving up on me
she already did when she silently kept giving me chances
to change
but i'd say sorry and move on like it was another new
day
but this time she had had enough
so i let her go
i stood there with a blank face staring into her
till i went blank and fell
i woke up to her gone for good
it was the same night yesterday
it's the same night tonight
it's been the same night for a while now —as along as i
can remember.

the spring is here
but for me it is still winter
dear love dear love
dear love

dear love
dear love——

———

—————

d—

hello,
I am Mark, not an unusual
name but my parents say i was dented—never
understood why. I hope we can be good friends.

TW. Merely a Victim

You torched my skin with a hot glass.
I whimpered like a bondage slave,
And something psychotic in you, smiled.
You liked my cries,
The face I made, like I was begging you for my life.
A sadistic pleasure woke in you.
You wanted to torture me to feel that adrenaline rush
again and again, and another time, and for a last time,
and forever.
So you took me to the basement, unconscious.
Let me loose near a chair, yet tied me up mentally,
Like I was to know where I belonged.
I belonged to you—
Not in a romantic, amorous way, but in a tormented,
lamenting way,
Like I was a piece of something, and my tears your prize.
More like my expression of grief,
The terror in my bloodshot eyes,
My contorted face in agony,
My brows furrowed by suffering,

And my twitching body in extreme disgust.
You like it.
I can see it in your eyes, your smirk;
I can read your mind clearer than ever.
You wanted a project for your experiment,
Not one that would serve a purpose for the good,
But to serve your devilish desires.
And I know why you like it all too well,
You feel the power in putting me down. There's pleasure
in hearing my voice weak and delicate,
And most of all, for being the predator rather than the
victim this time. I see courage in your eyes.
I know it all too well,
For I felt that power once too often with you tied down
in the basement.

TW. Im not sentimental but

This body feels sick, and it pains in every part that is
human.
My heart needs a hug,
The kind that's tight enough to feel loved and not
wanting to lose.
Her gut whispers, "Please stay, don't leave."
I know you are suffering, but when will I have the time
to think about me and not look selfish?
I wish I could cry out loud and put an end to the pain.
Knowing it wouldn't die, I strangled myself with a blue
dupatta.
I stayed like that for 15 minutes.
I woke up.

13. Intoxication

baby, *Irish liquor* runs on your lips
with a hint of lemon juice
baby *Irish liquor* runs in your veins
with a hint of orange venom

you got that *baileys* stuck on your teeth
i wish to suck on them like a weaning baby
this *Irish cocktail* i am so stuck upon
but babe you're no Irish man

you bit the vessels in my throat with your fangs
and now that *Irish liquor* runs in my blood.
now i'm all about that *Irish cocktail*
yeah i crave it every night and day

i know it runs in my body now
like you're under my skin but so far along.
now i'm an owl in this dark night
waiting for your bite once and for all.

salty valentine

a beautiful house with a front yard and a backyard
there's a fountain just a little ahead before the entrance
the yards are greener than ever
there are three house dogs
they run and play catch n throw
there's a fish pond outside and a fish tank inside the
house
they represent her or so she thinks
life is etched in her skin- the walls of this house
the heart beats, the bells ring every time there's someone
at the door
she rushes to the door- the bell was rung
the door is open now welcoming the cold wind
there is no stranger standing, there are no known lovers
knocking either
a familiar fragrance surrounds her hair
she had dreamt about for a couple of nights now
the bells ringing was in her head or so i thought
she stood at the door hoping someone would peekaboo
her, 'let it at least be a delivery guy' she thought to

herself

the wind grew louder and colder yet no one to be seen

click the door shuts and her heart sunk into a pit

she smiled as she walked into her kitchen

'salt' she yelled out 'it's in the sink'

there's a beige brown window right beside the sink

a white flash captures her attention

she glances back into the sink as the salt disappears in
the water

'oh dear i should pick that up or i'll lose all the salt, the
salt is getting wet(this feels good for some reason)' she
goes on while she stands watching the salt emptying
from the shaker

does she let it empty? or does she hold onto the little
honor left in her body?

every day is cold

I still remember that cold night,
when I thought that,
soon—on a cold night—I'd hug her,
and it would be warm and cozy again.
I'd sleep with everything forgotten,
just me, wrapped in her soft arms.
She would sing me our favorite lullabies
while I bathed in her warmth.
But now, all my nights have turned cold,
and I think of that night every day.

sweet 16

I see it.
I see her in the back of my mind, through my eyes—
when I look in the mirror or close my eyes.
It's not that I want to forget her,
but if I think about her now, it feels like I'll drown in her
—
through the windows of my eyes, I'll be trapped in the
back of my head, in her cage.
She isn't the cage that holds you back, but the one that
loves you and sets you free.
The real cage is my eye; it lets me look at all of it, and I
feel it all too well—
because that's the power of her love.
My eyes will tear up, and I'll never be able to swim
across it.
The tension in my eyes will push me, and the gravity of
her loss will pull me further in.
Maybe it's all in my head.
But isn't that the whole nature of this *tragedy*—
that I wish it was just the despair of a nightmare,

while in reality, she is right here, wrapped in my arms,
asking for hot chocolate?
How convenient, isn't it?
For me to live like she's just gone to the market.
She's at the market, buying veggies,
while I'm home, in the comfort of her sacrifices and hard
work.
I don't think about it, though...
I live in the fear that I'll remain alone forever,
because one day, I'll lose her too—against all my will.
I live in that fear for years.
Then I lose her. Forever, this time.
But she's still at the market, buying veggies, isn't she?
While I sleep in sadness, thinking I'm lonely.

the inevitable

I always knew that I'm going to be alone, I always told
myself to detach
because there won't be no one with me in the long run:
today I am actually alone and I had thought that I knew
how to survive
but today I really know what to be alone and lonely truly
meant.
Yesterday I could trust fall on her—
today I land stranded,
a third person in my own affairs,
I inevitably wish to escape this body.
Nothing holds meaning anymore but so does
everything.
There is no same time, there is no more of you
'physically' present for me to rely on.
There is none me mentally, present to fight long.
There is no more life in me today than there was
yesterday but only lesser
I have stopped counting the days or knowing the
difference between Sunday and Monday

or any day of the week for that matter
I am still in august.
no calendar can justify the date to me. no new year no
new no new no new anything,
but good old pain in a different back alley,
a dark knight with a sharper blade—a slyer way to
penetrate this numb skull.

TW - . please, I beg

My soul is being tortured, and I see you walking away.
I'm crying inside; these voices, they're pounding my
brain.
Will you stay? Will you be alive? Will you recover from
all the pain?
Will you leave me here to die? Will you go away? Far
away? To your father?
Will I be all alone again?
Drowning in Mariana's Trench,
My blood seeping all through my dying veins.
Why are you leaving me?
Please don't LEAVE ME!
I'll try to be a better daughter,
I'll try to be a better person,
I'll try to grow a heart from new,
I'll try to be the better version.
Please open your eyes.
Please come to me and hug my heart.
It's painful, and it's dying now,
Like a fish that jumped out of the water, gasping for air.

Don't leave me now.

I'll be there with you.

But just in case you choose to leave all of me—this
world behind,

Just remember that I'll follow you anywhere you go.

I'll sit at Heaven's gate for you,

I'll stand there now, welcoming you,

Only in case you let me go.

But don't let it go.

Keep this life inside your heart; let it grow all over your
life tonight.

Be happy and be blessed, and that God is healing every
inch.

That retropharyngeal abscess will disappear into
nothingness, and you'll be able to breathe again.

I love you, I do more than life, I love you.

More than the skies and the waters, and God, I love you.

Every day, I try my best to stay alive for you,

So don't leave me alone.

Please.

19 TW. ONCE AGAIN I AM HELPLESS

I'm staying strong like an old abandoned building.
I'm hopeful like that street dog waiting for their angelic
person to see them, waiting for a sign.
This feeling is everything, and yet hopelessly empty.
I once wished that we die together because I knew she
wouldn't survive without me, and I always wanted to
die.
To think whoever up there makes decisions took her
away from me when I am only 20.
I don't know what to respond to, 'Hey, how are you?'
Because the ground beneath my feet crumbles to ashes
when her dead face stands between me and the death I
always wanted.
Every time I think about the moments before her funeral,
my head starts to feel like it's going to explode. I feel
paralyzed, then, 'She wants me to be happy, she wants
me to live my life, I shouldn't make her sad like this'
pulls me to the brim of my reality.
I am back in my body.

Laughing at a joke my brother-in-law makes doesn't
make me want to suffocate myself.

But my conscience does. Whenever I smile or laugh, I
think to myself—*I should be shattered, I should be deeply
dying inside, I don't have the right to be laughing or
even smiling in fact.*

It's only been a week.

Everyone tells me to be strong, study well, 'we are there
for you na...'

No one says, '

No one looks me in the eye, pats my head, kisses my
forehead, and tells me "I am here na, my thangapilla," like
she did.

I always wanted to be there for her.

I wanted to make her happy and proud.

I wanted to give her a house filled with everything she
ever desired.

She wanted to enjoy, she wanted me to enjoy with her,
but she never asked that.

She always said, 'Don't look for company, be your own
company.'

But she always meant, 'I am your company; where are
you looking outside?'

I love her so much.

I want to love her and pet her for my whole life.

But thinking about her this way makes me feel like she
would be sad because I'm crying.

I have so many people to tell me to be strong.
But none who would hug me and just let me cry because
it hurts.
I'm numb, but it hurts.
My eyes burn from all the tears and wiping.
But there is so much work left to do.
I will stay strong for that.
I will stay strong for her.

20. Quiet Days

It's a new morning
A sip of my tea I take,
It's a refreshing start to the end of my week.

The longing's over
The tables are set for a new family in this house,
The clock I'll take down as the last thing from here on.

The view outside the window is different now
The rain is pretty today, she's taking my pain away,
Finally, I can put myself to *rest.*

Tomorrow will be a new day for you
The beginning of a new week,
Go forth my dear spread your love, *call your friends
over, tell your mom you love her.*

21. Change- a parting gift

people say 'do not change' but let me tell you otherwise,
if you feel a change in yourself and it's good then let it
change you to the best version of yourself.
let your love grow stronger for your heart and mind, for
your loved ones and for the world
let your mind move out of the box and into the streams
of a new realm
let your hands grow towards to show more compassion
for yourself first and for all the lessons and gifts this life
of yours has to give
let your feet run forward to risks and success and once
in a while allow yourself to take a step back not to see
where you started from but to feel every blessing and
love that carried you through and where you have now
come
let your ears grow wider for the knowledge of how pure
your existence is and will be
let your mouth open with joy and laughter and only for
wisdom of greatness even when it's for you

let your eyes see not just the greatness but also the love
and intentions of all the acts performed
let your nose smell the divinity that surrounds your
heart and the flowers of your garden
let the breeze flow through your hair and into your soul
let your self know what it feels like to run through a
field of green grass
let yourself just be there and soak the goodness of your
being and not just from the world.